D0116564

A New True Book

ZOOS

By Karen Jacobsen

This "true book" was prepared
under the direction of
Illa Podendorf,
formerly with the Laboratory School,
University of Chicago

CHILDRENS PRESS, CHICAGO

Siberian tiger

PHOTO CREDITS

David J. Maenza—Cover

Lynn M. Stone—2, 4 (top), 11 (2 photos), 14, 16 (top) 21 (top left, bottom left, and right), 23 (bottom), 27, 28 (bottom left), 30 (top), 34, 40 (middle and bottom), 42 (top)

Mark Rosenthal—4 (bottom), 12

Tony Freeman—6, 42 (bottom right)

James P. Rowan—8, 13, 16 (bottom), 19, 23 (top), 24 (2 photos), 26, 28 (top, bottom right), 30 (bottom), 33, 35, 36 (2 photos, at right), 38 (top), 40 (top), 42 (bottom left), 44 (3 photos)

Jerry Hennen—21 (top right)

Root Resources—© Anthony Mercieca, 32

Allan Roberts—36 (top, left), 38 (bottom)

COVER—A view of Lincoln Park Zoo, Chicago

Library of Congress Cataloging in Publication Data

Jacobsen, Karen.
  Zoos.

  (A New true book)
  Summary: An introduction to zoos and the animals that live in them, including the elephant, rhinoceros, giraffe, antelope, lion and giant panda.
  1. Zoo animals—Juvenile literature.
2. Zoological gardens—Juvenile literature.
[1. Zoo animals. 2. Zoological gardens]
I. Title.
QL77.5.J3   1982   590'.74'4   82-9545
ISBN 0-516-01664-4   AACR2

TABLE OF CONTENTS

Sea lions and seals like water.

ZOO ANIMALS

There is much to see
while at a zoo
   You watch the animals...
and they watch you!
   Many wonderful animals
live in a zoo. The zoo is
their home.
   Some of the animals
were born in the zoo. But
most zoo animals come
from faraway places.

African elephant

ELEPHANTS

This mother elephant is from Africa. But her baby was born in a zoo.

At night and when it is cold elephants live inside a large building.

On nice days they stay outside.

Elephants are the largest land animals in the world.

In Africa elephants eat leaves, roots, grass, and fruit. They have to find all their own food.

In zoos elephants eat lots of hay, grain, and fruit every day.

Mame, an African elephant, does a trick for her keeper.

Elephants love water.

Sometimes an elephant uses its trunk to take a shower—or to give one to someone else.

Keepers take care of the elephants.

Every day the keepers clean the elephant house and yard. Then they wash everything—even the elephants.

RHINOCEROS AND HIPPOPOTAMUS

The rhinoceros is from Africa.

An adult rhinoceros, or rhino, weighs over four thousand pounds. Even so, a rhino can run very fast.

A rhino has tough, thick skin. It has two sharp horns on its head. Rhinos use their horns as weapons.

Rhinoceroses are dangerous in the wild and in zoos.

The hippopotamus is as big as a rhinoceros. It also comes from Africa.

Hippos like water. They can hold their breath and stay underwater for ten minutes or more.

Pigmy hippopotamus

In Africa hippos eat wild water plants.

In the zoo hippos eat hay and grain. They like fruit and vegetables, too.

13

Giraffes cannot bend their necks. Giraffes must spread their
front legs apart in order to lower their heads to drink water
from a river.

GIRAFFES

Giraffes are the tallest animals in the world.

They have long legs and very long necks. They use their extra long tongues to pluck leaves from trees.

In a zoo, giraffes eat hay, grain, fruit, and vegetables.

Camels usually live in dry, desert places.

CAMELS

There are two kinds of camels. African camels have one hump on their backs. Asiatic camels have two humps.

The humps are used to store fat. Well-fed camels have big humps. Hungry camels have small humps. If they must, camels can go for a long time without food or water.

ZEBRAS

Zebras belong to the horse family. They live in herds in the wild.

There are not many wild zebras left. They need lots of open grassland to live. But people make farms on the grassland.

In zoos zebras can get food and live in safety.

Grant's zebra

ANTELOPES AND DEER

There are dozens of different kinds of antelopes in the world.

Antelopes are very close relatives of deer.

Antelopes come in many different sizes. Some are very small. Others are quite large.

Antelopes are grazing animals. They travel in herds.

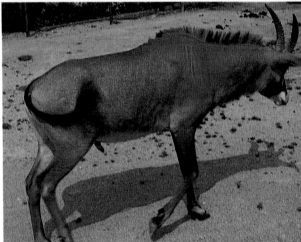

Above left: Black buck
Above right: Pronghorn antelope
Left: Gazelle
Above: Oryx

They are fast runners
and can jump very high.

THE BIG CATS

Lions, tigers, and leopards are all members of the cat family. They all have fur, sharp claws and teeth, and long tails.

Big cats eat meat. In the wild they are good hunters. But they kill only what they need to eat.

In zoos, lions live in the open. They have a house to go into at night and in bad weather.

African lions

Male lions have a mane.

A lion baby is called a cub.

Lions like to live in family groups called prides. There are usually males and females and some young cubs in a pride.

All of the lions look after each other. In the wild they share their food. In the zoo each animal receives a portion of meat for itself.

Tara, a Siberian tiger

Tigers are very big cats.
Tigers can weigh more
and are usually longer than
lions.

Tigers do not live
together in groups. They
like to hunt alone at night.

They are very good
swimmers.

Snow leopard

Leopards are smaller than lions and tigers. But they are fast runners.

In the jungle, leopards climb trees. In the zoo, they like to sit up high on a perch, so they can watch everyone and everything.

Top: Kodiak bear
Above left: Black bear
Right: Brown bear

BEARS

Many zoos have bears. Black bears come from North America. Some are black, but others are brown, cinnamon, or even blonde.

Black bears are meat and fish eaters. They also like berries and honey.

In a zoo, bears need a lot of room to climb and walk around.

Polar bears have white coats. They are hard to see in the snow of the North Pole.

Polar bears come from the North Pole where it is cold and icy.

In the wild, polar bears hunt seals and catch fish.

In the zoo, they eat frozen fish and horse meat.

To stay healthy, polar bears need a big pool for swimming.

Giant panda. All pandas eat bamboo shoots.

Giant pandas look like bears, but they are not bears. They come from China and Tibet.

Pandas are rare in nature, and there are very few pandas in zoos.

Gorillas eat fruit and vegetables.

APES AND MONKEYS

Of all the animals in the zoo, apes are the most like people.

Gorillas are the largest and strongest apes. They are smart and very gentle.

Orangutans use
their long arms
to swing from
place to place.

Orangutans are also
large apes. Their bodies
are round and they have
very long arms.

Mibuti, a chimpanzee

Chimpanzees are smaller apes. They are very clever and love to do tricks.

Top: Monkeys looking for
peanuts.
Above left: Squirrel monkey
eating an insect.
Above right: Owl monkeys
Right: Rhesus monkey

There are dozens of kinds of monkeys in the world. They come from Africa, Asia, and South America.

Monkeys like to eat fruit and vegetables.

Sometimes monkeys are very quiet. Other times they race around and make a lot of noise.

South American tree boa

Broad-banded copperhead

REPTILES

Reptiles, from near and far away, live at many zoos. There are hundreds, even thousands, of different kinds of reptiles.

Snakes are reptiles.

Some snakes are poisonous. Others are not. People like to watch snakes.

Above: American
alligator
Right: Close-up of
a crocodile's
mouth
Below: These turtles
live in water. All
turtles have shells.

Alligators and crocodiles are the largest reptiles.

They can stay underwater for a long time, but they must breathe air.

Alligators and crocodiles eat fish, birds, and other animals. They can be very dangerous to people.

Turtles are reptiles, too. They come in all sizes.

Many turtles live in or near water, but some live in the desert.

Top: Penguins
Above left: Peacock
Right: Flamingo

BIRDS

Birds are popular zoo animals.

Most penguins live around the South Pole.

Penguins cannot fly. On the ground they are slow movers. But they can swim very fast.

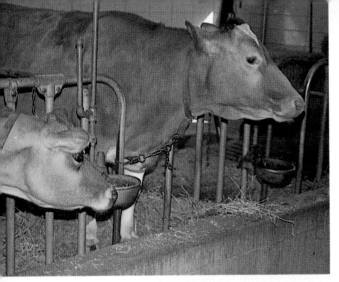

Above left: Cows
Above right:
Dairy barn
Right: Horses

Today many zoos keep
cows, pigs, goats, sheep,
and rabbits. Farm animals
are very gentle.

A zoo is a home for all kinds of animals. It is a wonderful place to visit.

When you are at the zoo, be quiet and look very closely. Watch the animals and learn about them. Then you will see the animals as they really are.

WORDS YOU SHOULD KNOW

alert(ah • LIRT) — watchful; to be aware
antler(ANT • ler) — a bony growth on the head of some animals
bamboo(bam • BOO) — a tall grass that looks like a tree
brilliant(BRILL • yant) — shining; very bright
clever(KLEH • ver) — having a quick mind; smart
coarse(KORSE) — not smooth; rough
dangerous(DAINJ • er • us) — full of harm; risky
desert(DEZ • ert) — a dry region usually covered with sand
favorite(FAVE • er • it) — liked best
grain(GRANE) — the seeds of wheat, corn, rice, and other cereal
      plants
grazing(GRAY • zing) — to feed on grass
herd(HIRD) — a group of animals that stays together
keeper(KEEP • er) — a person who takes care of an animal
mane(MAIN) — the long hair that grows from the neck and head of
      some animals
orangutan(or • ANG • gih • tan) — a large ape that has long arms
      and shaggy reddish-brown hair
pace(PAISS) — to walk back and forth
pluck(PLUK) — to pick
pride(PRYDE) — the name given for a lion group
rare(RAIR) — not usual; special
reptile(REP • tile) — a group of cold-blooded animals with
      backbones that contains snakes, turtles, and lizards
shed — to lose; drop
temper(TEM • per) — state of mind; mood
Tibet(tih • BET) — a country in Asia
weapon(WEP • un) — something used to attack another or defend
      oneself from attack
wild — growing, living, or found in a natural state.

INDEX

About the Author

Karen Jacobsen is a graduate of the University of Connecticut and Syracuse University. She has been a teacher and is a writer. She likes to find out about interesting subjects and then write about them.